ENDURE

Look to the Lion & the Lamb

Jill Deville

Show What You Know

Jill Deville

ISBN : 9798329475913 (Paperback)

Copyright © 2024 Jill Deville
All Rights Reserved
First Edition

All rights reserved. No part of this publication may be reproduced, distributed, or transmitted in any form or by any means, including photocopying, recording, or other electronic or mechanical methods without the prior written permission of the publisher. For permission requests, solicit the publisher via the address below.

Jill L Deville
P.O. BOX 876
Basile, La 70515
JillDevilleWorldMinistry@gmail.com
www.JillDevilleWorldMinistry.com

Dear Reader

I pray this book will help you in many ways to understand why we endure so much. The Story of Joseph taught me what we achieve when we endure. What stood out most to me was found in Genesis 50:19-21, that everything that was meant to hurt us, God turns to our good and for the good of many. Every single moment in our lives is an invite to get closer and closer to God as we walk from faith to faith. Thank you for trusting in me to share what God has done in me, for me, and through me, I pray it gives you hope. Thank you for support, and time. I truly appreciate you and would love to hear from you.

Author, Jill Deville

JillDevilleWorldMinistry@gmail.com

Jill Deville

1 Corinthians 10:13 Amplified Bible No temptation [regardless of its source] has overtaken or enticed you that is not common to human experience [nor is any temptation unusual or beyond human resistance]; but God is faithful [to His word—He is compassionate and trustworthy], and He will not let you be tempted beyond your ability [to resist], but along with the temptation He [has in the past and is now and] will [always] provide the way out as well, so that you will be able to endure it [without yielding, and will overcome temptation with joy].

CONTENTS

Introduction		7
Chapter 1:	Temptation	14
Chapter 2:	Mount Up	22
Chapter 3	Be Steadfast	29
Chapter 4	Traditions	36
Chapter 5	Consider it Joy	44
Chapter 6	Be The Image Of Christ	50
Chapter 7	Your Identity	59
Chapter 8	Focus On The Race	67
Chapter 9	Do Not Give Up	77
Chapter 10	Finish The Race	84
About the Author		90
Other Titles		93

Jill Deville

INTRODUCTION

Your heart is racing, breath shattered, tears rolling down your face, and that overwhelming feeling that you have just been backed into a corner with the news flooding your mind. Whether it is the news of a loved one, illness, relationship, or a bill that has arrived, here you are in wonder or position with the thought or the action, "Am I ready or not?"

Maybe you are the one that anger is raging through you in your first reaction. You feel your fist balling up, you have the urge to hit something or someone just to feel in control, or you have just blurted out a series of words or raised your voice. This may allow you to believe that you have taken charge of the matter for the moment. Did it help, really? You wonder or maybe you do not even consider that in all actuality it has only released a little pressure, a temporary fix to give you a moment to contemplate your next move.

My prayer is that this book and all that I have endured in the past two years through four brain suregeries, is that Jesus can get you to a reaction in faith that says, " **Satan you picked the wrong one, Are you ready or not??, because here Jesus and I come**!"

It is time you know your access, position, and title in Christ. It is time that all the training you have endured to be utilized to walk in faith and no longer grow weary or angry. For too long the enemy has convinced you that you were in fear, weak, or not able. For too long the enemy has convinced you to be tuff to not allow anyone else to mess with you. Now you will know the truth and the truth will set you free.

Once we realize the one and only reason we are under attack, or temptation of any kind, then we begin to take it as a compliment, a challenge, a task for the good for us and many others like Joseph in Genesis 50: 19-21.

Genesis 50:19-21 Amplified Bible [19] But Joseph said to them, "Do not be afraid, for am I in the place of God? [Vengeance is His, not mine.] [20] As for you, you meant evil against me, but God meant it for good in order to bring about this present outcome, that many people would be kept alive [as they are this day]. [21] So now, do not be afraid; I will provide for you and support you and your little ones." So he comforted them [giving them encouragement and hope] and spoke [with kindness] to their hearts.

If you are familiar with Joseph, many see him as a man of great faith, access, and power in Christ. However, if you truly consider Joseph and his story in its entirety you will realize that faith, access, and power in Christ came from endurance. Consider Joseph as that little boy favored by his father but hated and rejected by his brothers. Consider Joseph sold to strangers by his own family, to be that young man that thought, " I will never see my father again." Consider Joseph when he was put in jail due to lies when he was being so faithful to his leader and to God. Consider all the places God allowed Joseph to go was training him, molding him, and producing such an endurance in him that allowed him to be the leader he turned out to be.

The things Joseph went through, the things he endured allowed him to learn about the people, the surroundings, the culture, the languages, the process from the inside out. More importantly it built a bond between him and God that was so unbreakable that you could not convince Joseph to put anyone or anything before God. So that when God put him in the leadership position, he promised all along in the dream at such a young age, Joseph was ready. Joesph new the importance and he would not fail God, himself or all the people God trusted him with. You see without that endurance Joseph could have become any of the enemies that he was faced with. Because Joseph new how those people, places and things came against him, Joseph gained wisdom, understanding, faith, hope, love, kindness, mercy, goodness, self-control, peace, patience, and forgiveness.

Joseph was not that strong, however the one living in Joseph was! We just need to be reminded that God is in us and working through us when we give Him the access.

2 Corinthians 6: 16- 18 Amp 16 What agreement is there between the temple of God and idols? For we are the temple of the living God; just as God said: "I will dwell among them and walk among them; And I will be their God, and they shall be My people. 17 "So come out from among unbelievers and be separate," says the Lord, "And do not touch what is unclean; And I will graciously receive you and welcome you [with favor], 18 And I will be a Father to you, And you will be My sons and daughters," Says the Lord Almighty.

I love that readers love the books that God and I write together; our prayer is that these books intrigue you to read the word of God more to get to know your family in Christ. What they endured, what they stood for, and how they relate to you. This will help you in every part of your life to know that you are not defeated, it is not impossible, you are not a mess. God choose you and He is using every single part of our lives to give others hope through our growth and testimony. He done the hard part, He paid the price. Jesus Christ died on the cross for you and I to be set free from the sin that has tricked us, distracted us, confused us, and intrigued us. Jesus Christ gave up His fleshy life at the age of thirty-three for you and me. Can we give up our fleshy ways for Him? This will not only save us and turn things for our good. It will turn things for the good of many. Joseph showed us this.

In the book of Revelations 12 God shares this important message for us to understand our flesh in sacrifice is just as important as the sacrifice Jesus Christ made for us. For Jesus Christ, He gave all of His flesh to walk in the spirit with us all the days of our lives. For us He just wants us to surrender the sin in the flesh to walk as evidence of Him as ambassadors of Christ. Look how powerful your breakthrough is here:

Revelations 12: 10-12 Amplified Bible 10 *Then I heard a loud voice in heaven, saying, "Now the salvation, and the power, and the kingdom (dominion, reign) of our God, and the authority of His Christ have come; for the [e]accuser of our [believing] brothers and sisters has been thrown down [at last], he who accuses them and keeps bringing charges [of sinful behavior] against them before our God day and night.* **11** *And they overcame and conquered him <u>because of the blood of the Lamb</u> <u>and</u> <u>because of the word of their testimony</u>, for they did not love their life and renounce their faith even when faced with death.* **12** *Therefore rejoice, O heavens and you who dwell in them [in the presence of God]. Woe to the earth and the sea, because the devil has come down to you in great wrath, knowing that he has only a short time [remaining]!"*

Jill Deville

Let me encourage you to activate the word of God within you get in the word of God, and learn more about Joseph:

*Joseph's story is told in **Genesis** (37–50). Joseph, most beloved of Jacob's sons, is hated by his envious brothers. Angry and jealous of Jacob's gift to Joseph, a resplendent "coat of many colors," the brothers seize him and sell him to a party of Ishmaelites, or Midianites, who carry him to Egypt. When you focus on the faith Joseph had most often you do not consider the endurance that it all came with. Meet Joseph, and meet yourself. The one that is a fighter from within, the one that trust in the Lord more than you realize.*

Take this section to tell your older self what you received in this intro and let me encourage you to take notes of what stood out to you that God used, or could use for the good of not only you, but many others as you read this book, and the book of Joseph. I pray wisdom, understanding over you in the name of Jesus. I pray as you read this book and the story of Joseph you see the message, the hope, the instructions, and the example Jesus Christ left for you in Joseph that will now carry on to all that meet you in Jesus' name amen.

ENDURE

CHAPTER 1

Temptation

1 Corinthians 10:13 Amplified Bible No temptation [regardless of its source] has overtaken or enticed you that is not common to human experience [nor is any temptation unusual or beyond human resistance]; but God is faithful [to His word—He is compassionate and trustworthy], and He will not let you be tempted beyond your ability [to resist], but along with the temptation He [has in the past and is now and] will [always] provide the way out as well, so that you will be able to endure it [without yielding, and will overcome temptation with joy].

Temptation comes from all sorts of ways. We often do not even consider it a temptation at first. Temptation can come from the person that randomly texts something so inconsiderate, selfish, condescending, arrogant, or manipulative. Temptation can come from

ENDURE

a pair of shoes that just so happened to pop up right when you looked on your phone. Temptation can come from comments from a loved one or an enemy. Temptation can come from commercials with a juicy burger or delicious ice cream with all the toppings. The Temptation comes from seeing socials where it appears others are prospering with Jesus, relationships, work, school, or friends. Temptation is not always the poisonous apple that Adam, Eve or Snow White was tempted with.

    The devil is out to distract you, attack you, tempt you, play with you, he really has no preference. The devil does not mind sharing you with God at all. He will watch you walk right into that church every Sunday and cause you to look like a fool while you there, on the way there or the moment you leave. How? He will have somone sit in your seat. He will have someone take too long to get dressed. He will have somone slam on the breaks in front of you. He will tempt you with a song that has nothing to do with Jesus on your way to or from church, causing you to reminisce on the ungodly days. Your keys will be missing. He will bring up conversations in church with others to tempt you to talk about them and not pray for them. He will show you things your pastor or church members done to have you judge them. Am I the only one?

    The word of God teaches us that the devil prowls around like a lion seeking whom he may devour. I want you to really think of this verse. You will find a secret in the word whom! He can only have access if you give it to him. That is what 1 Corinthians 10:13 is also teaching us. You see the same situations mentioned above can also be paths of endurance, a gift from God to teach, guide and remind you. Let's take a look at it.

Getting to church and seeing someone in your seat at church should not bother you, it should show you that you have grown because you are glad to see that new or existing person in church seeking the Lord. When tempted with your child, parent, spouse taking to long to get in the car for church, is this teaching you how to consider others, is it teaching you patience? Are you thinking back to when they did not want to go to church at all? Is your judgment from when you did this to your parents? Use the training you have to say I discern you taking to long because you do not want to go. Get ready and be in the car or you will go unprepared, if you are the parent. If you are the spouse stand firm in your faith and tell Jesus what they are doing and trust me, he will get on to them and you will see them jump in that car. When you choose to seek God first even in this by saying Lord, help me. You are showing God you trust in Him you need Him, you are operating in your faith, and you are waiting on the Lord. This may take a few Sundays because you may need a little help in the patience department.

ENDURE

We get the choice to have wisdom and understanding that everything works out for our good and the good of others with an action. Or we have the choice to be tempted by the devil and act and react like him. The choice is yours 1 Corinthians 10:13 says we have a choice. Will we decide to be the ambassador of Christ to heal and be healed with endurance, or will we decide to operate like the devil and hurt and be hurt.

1 Peter 5: 1- 11 Amplified Bible Serve God Willingly
5 Therefore, I strongly urge the elders among you [pastors, spiritual leaders of the church], as a fellow elder and as an eyewitness [called to testify] of the sufferings of Christ, as well as one who shares in the glory that is to be revealed: ² shepherd and guide and protect the flock of God among you, exercising oversight not under compulsion, but voluntarily, according to the will of God; and not [motivated] for shameful gain, but with wholehearted enthusiasm; ³ not lording it over those assigned to your care [do not be arrogant or overbearing], but be examples [of Christian living] to the flock [set a pattern of integrity for your congregation]. ⁴ And when the Chief Shepherd (Christ) appears, you will receive the [conqueror's] unfading crown of glory. ⁵ Likewise, you younger men [of lesser rank and experience], be subject to your elders [seek their counsel]; and all of you, clothe yourselves with

humility toward one another [tie on the servant's apron], for GOD IS OPPOSED TO THE PROUD *[the disdainful, the presumptuous, and He defeats them],* BUT HE GIVES GRACE TO THE HUMBLE. *⁶Therefore humble yourselves under the mighty hand of God [set aside self-righteous pride], so that He may exalt you [to a place of honor in His service] at the appropriate time, ⁷casting all your cares [all your anxieties, all your worries, and all your concerns, once and for all] on Him, for He cares about you [with deepest affection, and watches over you very carefully]. ⁸Be sober [well balanced and self-disciplined], be alert and cautious at all times. That enemy of yours, the devil, prowls around like a roaring lion [fiercely hungry], seeking someone to devour. ⁹But resist him, be firm in your faith [against his attack— rooted, established, immovable], knowing that the same experiences of suffering are being experienced by your brothers and sisters throughout the world. [You do not suffer alone.] ¹⁰After you have suffered for a little while, the God of all grace [who imparts His blessing and favor], who called you to His own eternal glory in Christ, will Himself complete, confirm, strengthen, and establish you [making you what you ought to be]. ¹¹To Him be dominion (power, authority, sovereignty) forever and ever. Amen.*

ENDURE

For this book I went with the amplified version for the verses shared to help break down the verses more to open the door wide for us to explore all that God has for us. As Christians we will not say, "I done this because he or she done this." We will learn to say, "I done this because He (JESUS) said." What God shows me in my life is to use the endurance, the training, the evidence God gave me and share this with you in my books, so that through my journey without Him and with Him you will have evidence of hope that when you decide to seek Christ first and His right standing all will be added to you, not until then.

When we begin to see any and every situation in the power and authority of Jesus Christ our view, access, opinions, faith, opportunities, and circumstances change. For to long we take on things as an attack to us as if it has power and authority over us. But when you learn from the Lord that these people, places, and things have no power over you unless you allow them to, then things change, traditions change, your knowing changes, and you begin to be the living breathing example of Christ to others. When they see things happening in your life because of your faith in Christ. There is no way to deny that it is Christ Jesus in you, that is powering you up.

Decide to Show What You Know!

Jill Deville

Ask Jesus to expose what tempts you. Ask Jesus to expose

how easy it tempts you. Then ask Jesus to remind, teach and guide you through it with wisdom, understanding, discernment, courage, power and authority to resist what tempts you.

Take note of the things that tempt you so that now that you expose (admit and reveal them) you can look back and not only be hope to others but begin your journey in seeing how much you have grown and how much you are growing daily.

I expose you in Jesus Name and I am trading you for freedom in Jesus name amen.

ENDURE

CHAPTER 2

Mount Up

Isaiah 40:31 Amplified Bible ³¹ But those who wait for the LORD [who expect, look for, and hope in Him]Will gain new strength and renew their power; They will lift up their wings [and rise up close to God] like eagles [rising toward the sun]; They will run and not become weary, They will walk and not grow tired.

Waiting on the Lord is not always that easy. Especially in today's world, where we want what we want, and we want it right now. We may think it all began with something like fast food instead of purchasing the food, then going home to unload the food, then cooking and serving the food. We may think it started from the microwave verses standing over the food and cooking it. However, it started with as simple as a seed. You know the one. Where the packet of seeds verses waiting on the process of the previous harvest to dry and provide the new harvest.

ENDURE

In our natural mind when we need to wait in line for a burger let's face it we get impatient. But we can overcome that. When we learn to be trusted with the little waits, when we endure in the simple waits, then we can look from faith to faith and grow in the long-suffering waits. You may be thinking, how can waiting for food have anything to do with my faith system. Jesus has so much mercy and grace for us, that He must teach us in small doses how to wait. Just like He taught Joseph? No, Joseph was stronger and more prepared for what he was going to endure. We have been brought up in a "have it your way" manner even in the worse conditions and we need to endure even in the preparation of our faith.

You see we look at a long line and we often feel angry, selfish, inpatient, and we act on it. God teaches us in our anger do not sin therefore we can only discern in our worry, do not sin. When we are inpatient do not sin. When we get fearful, or confused, do not sin. Easy to say, hard to do, right? Especially when everyone else is reacting in this so-called natural way. Do you go as for as to justify yourself, or your sin by saying God made me this way, people are selfish, they are so inconsiderate, they need to move faster because I am here, and I am busy. What works for you? What causes you to feel like you are okay, and not in sin. Are you this easy to mess with? Does the devil know you can be distracted this easily? Or do you take power and authority in it and serve the Lord and produce patience, integrity, honor, and self-control?

I often say it will not be murder, stealing, cheating that will send many to hell. Most are aware of these harsh sins and become humble and sincerely ask for forgiveness when they sin in these ways. It is the constant gossip, anger, impatience, unforgiveness, selfishness, pride, and hate that many Christians of all walks of life do with no regret daily. Many are in the stage of justifications and excuses. Many simply have passed that stage and just do it, and feel that their attendance, appearance, and works excuse this. Then there are the ones that do, and say I need to stop with no intention on an action to back that up. Then there are the others with the pity party or pride thinking somehow, someway that excuses their sin.

When we decide and discern that change is needed for us to be set free we become like that eagle ready to take charge. We decide that our lives and the lives of the ones God has placed in our path are worth it. We begin to see and seek that we matter, and they do too. You see many of us care for our loved ones or ourselves to have the best clothes, or clothes at all. The best jobs or just a job to get by. The best food or food to just make sure we eat. But we often to not ensure we are fed and feed those the word of God with an action. We need to learn to mount up and get on that mountain.

Did you know when an eagle has their babies, they prepare that nest before they lay the eggs. They make sure it has the best foundation with sticks and thorns to bond it well, then they look for the softer materials for the eggs to set then hatch in a loving welcoming, comforting environment. Once hatched they feed them until they are mature enough to feed themselves. They act on position, and rank with the power, authority and wisdom that God gave them. They begin to take the soft materials away from the nest to cause discomfort and growth. This allows the babies to not get comfortable and begin to desire change. The discomfort helps encourage the transition. Then when the time comes the mother pushes them out of the nest to teach them to fly. They must learn in that instant to take the gift God gave them and fly or else they will fall to their death.

We are a lot like this as Christians we are meant to mount up and decide to fly. At first God allows the sticks and thorns to get us to that stage to become the egg and hatch for Him. Then we are fed by Him and those He trust to feed us. Then the time arrives to mount up and be pushed to fly. We are meant to rise and do what we are called to do. We are meant to take the gift, the ability, the information, the food, the knowledge and soar like an eagle.

The long line at the store, restaurants, hold times, and more are God's gift of mercy and grace in its beginning stages to help us to grow from faith to faith. If we can be trusted with the little, we can then be trusted with the lots. He says so in the book of Luke.

Luke 16:10 Amplified Bible **¹⁰** *"He who is faithful in a very little thing is also faithful in much; and he who is dishonest in a very little thing is also dishonest in much.*

Most of us have the crash course that sends us soaring right to the plunge of our death due to generational curses, the families we are born into or the circumstances we put ourselves in. Even then Jesus reminds us in 1 Corinthians 10:13 in Chapter one, that He is not tempting us with good or evil. He gives the way through it. Of course, most of us do not have parents that know better, to teach better. We cannot use this as an excuse, we cannot use this to be deserving. We need to use even this as training, hope, and our fight song!

Romans 1:16-17 Amplified Bible **¹⁶** *I am not ashamed of the gospel, for it is the power of God for salvation [from His wrath and punishment] to everyone who believes [in Christ as Savior], to the Jew first and also to the Greek.* **¹⁷** *For in the gospel the righteousness of God is revealed, both springing from faith and leading to faith [disclosed in a way that awakens more faith]. As it is written and forever remains written, "The just and upright shall live by faith."*

Take an inventory of what God has already gotten you

ENDURE

through. Maybe it was a huge or simple illness. Maybe it was a marriage. Maybe it was a test at school, training at work, or a challenge with finances. Take that and hold on to it as your evidence that God can, God did, God will, and God is. This is how you live faith to faith. Ask God to reveal your faith to you in your actions and reactions. You will begin to have more discernment on how strong or how weak your faith is. God wants the same faith you give your feet when you get out of bed, knowing they will hold you up. He wants the same faith you give your friends, parents, pastor, or spouse when you go to them for help, prayer, to have fun, to listen, or be listened to. God wants the same faith you give your car when you crank it, or the light switch when you turn it on. You believe in those people, places, and things when you go to them with an action. Maybe the only reason your faith is not on, is because you did not go to it, stand on it, turn it on, or crank it up. Let's reveal this to heal this now in Jesus' name amen.

Jill Deville

CHAPTER 3

Be Steadfast

1 Corinthians 15:58 Amplified Bible ⁵⁸ Therefore, my beloved brothers and sisters, be steadfast, immovable, always excelling in the work of the Lord [always doing your best and doing more than is needed], being continually aware that your labor [even to the point of exhaustion] in the Lord is not futile nor wasted [it is never without purpose].

Do you often feel like you are in a juggling match. You can be a great person at work, or at church but at home you have no respect, routine, or peace. Do you often feel like strangers understand you more than your own parents, children, siblings, or friends?

This often is because we will give our all where it is needed and appreciated in a place where we can grow, be noticed, achieve goals, accolades, awards, positions and more. Then we push aside the areas that we feel we will not meet or reach expectations in.

Sorry we need the truth to be set free, right? This is not always the case. Some of us want to be that great sister, brother, spouse, mom, dad, friend but no matter how hard we try, or how much we have changed we still are scene as that little child, that person that failed or mess up, that sinner, addict, adulterer, thief and so on.

Some say we do not work, give, do, or show up for the attention, reward, acknowledgment or harvest. Once and awhile, this is genuinely true. Do you want to know how you will truly know if this is true? Do you want to be sanctified from this and know for sure? Remember we want to break generational curses, tradition, religion and we want to endure to persevere, amen? So here we go.

When you fall sick, and there is not a call from the person or persons that you always are there for, how does this make you feel? Do you discern and endure it with wisdom and understanding that Jesus Christ said what you do for me, I see you, and I will give you. Well Jesus, where are they so I can see you in them? He did not say we would reap it from the person we sow it into. He said we would reap what we sow by working for Him as a vessel to reach who, what, and when He needs us. So, if you are operating with a pure heart as a vessel for Jesus then you would not be looking for that specific person to give it back to you. When He allows that person, place or thing to be distracted and not come to your beck and call because you are at their beck and call in obedience to Him, not them. This is meant to heal you and reveal to you that you are sanctified and working for Him with a purely focused heart not looking to gain from the person, place, or thing you sow in to. You are looking at Him. You are working for Him.

What should be a celebration of our growth that happens in our heart and mind, often is easily tempted by that devil prowling around seeking whom He can devour with your feelings. Do not let Him. Take the victory lap and endure knowing God will send a stranger, or a person that you earned nothing with, that you did nothing for to walk in, to text, to give, to cook, to show up so that you also will know *JESUS JUST WALKED IN, CHECKED ON, AND IS THERE FOR YOU, HIS CHILD!* Do you receive this in Jesus' name. More importantly can you strive to act and react in this endurance and receive the reward from Jesus Christ? The one he promises us in Matthew 6!

When you have those moments of breakthrough, prayer, thanksgiving, worship, and sincere salvation. Your heart sends out prayers to Jesus. Those prayers sound allot like this, *"Lord take all that is not of you and make me more like you. Lord set me free and heal me from the things that distract me from you. Lord help me to be the example of you, so that others can see and meet you in me. Lord give me things that I can do for you. Lord heal me from this illness, marriage, friendship, finances, bondage, addiction, loneliness, lack of patience, lack of peace, heartache, pride, anger..."* and the list goes on. It is like an outpouring in that moment when you truly mean it. When that prayer is released in that type of outpouring God does not forget that prayer. The problem is you may forget that prayer.

He goes to work for you. He begins to assign angels, servants, locations to go to work for you. To go to battle for you. To listen for you. To help you. To support you. To be an example to you. Your plans that He spoke of to prosper, and succeed for a hope and a future was just activated! All of a sudden you start to see a huge shift in your life, and you begin to give credit to the devil for an attack when in all honesty Jesus is at war for your prayer to be answered.

Stop giving attention, power, and authority to somone you do not know, nor want to know, nor that has any relation or power over you. Decide you are a child of God. Decide that you are aware that nothing happens without God's approval and your acceptance to the invitation. God showed us this with Daniel, Job, Joseph, David, Ester, Deborah, Mary and so many more. If you take the time to get in the Word of God, you will get to know your family in Christ and you will

ENDURE

get to know the instructions, directions, promises, protection, provision and receive the very road map home.

You are more than a conqueror God says so. You can be that mother, father, friend, grandmother, sister, brother, wife, husband that the devil has convinced you that you are not. You can be the provider, and one to excel in your job, opportunities, dreams, and hopes that the devil has talked you out of due to change or fear. You gain access in your endurance through faith. Nothing that comes easy is ever remembered or appreciated. But those things you endured they power you up to persevere and be the person you were called to be.

Take everything back that the devil stole from you because you allowed him to. It is yours and at any moment you can and will take it back. Make him tremble when you get up for a change. Victory is yours in Jesus Christ. If you believe in the scriptures, if you believe what God says is true. If you believe in God, then you will show it in an action and reaction. It looks like this; the Lord is my Shephard I shall not want. Meaning when you are in want or need of anything at all, you seek Him first and His right standing, and all will be added to you. He promises you this in Psalms 23:1 and Matthew 6:33.

You have seen the verse that says the Lord will fight for you, you need only to be still. But yet you go, and you put up walls, you shout in defense, you try to rally a group to agree or defend you. That is not faith. Faith activated is you being still and seeking God first asking Him will you hand me the sling shot like you did for David or do you got this like you have done for Daniel. Stop grabbing the weapons of the devil to win a war that has nothing to do with the flesh. This is all distractions, illusions, and bait to tempt you from your promises, protection, plans, purpose, and promise land. Are you going to allow it? Or will endure and persevere through it! Decide to believe with action. Decide to take charge with an action. Decide that the only thing you fear is being left by God. That will change everything for you.

Take an inventory of what you trust in, and what you do things for. Ask God do I do this for you, or do I do this for me. Ask God do I show you that I believe in you with action, or reaction. Ask God to have the Holy Spirit guide you, teach you, and remind you of all that you need to know when you need to know it and do it.

ENDURE

CHAPTER 4

Traditions

2 Thessalonians 2:15 Amplified Bible **15** *So then, [a]brothers and sisters, stand firm and hold [tightly] to the traditions which you were taught, whether by word of mouth or by letter from us.*

When you think of traditions most people think of sports, holidays, religion, clothing, church, decorations, positions, businesses, meals, and things like that. Here Jesus is teaching us that the tradition is the example He left for us. The bread of life that is found in the Word of God. The example of the true way, truth and life that is found in the examples, and lives of the people in the bible, our true family tree. He has left us with the tree of life, not the tree of temptation.

When you get to know your family from the Old and New

ENDURE

Testament you see the people, places and things that God chooses to work with Him, and for Him. You get to see what their lives were like without Him and with Him. You get to see where God met them at. You get to see how God reached them in visions, dreams, through endurance, battles, sermons, and example. You get to see the way, the truth, and the life which is Jesus Christ in full action from His birth to His Ascending to Heaven in the Book of Matthew. You literally can meet Jesus Christ there in that book.

Reading the book of the Gospels is like finding the very journal, love letter, promises, access, thoughts, and evidence of what Jesus wants you to know. It is so personal, so exciting, so raw, so true, so activated. It is the one and only way to access everything from Jesus Christ. By reading the book of Matthew you get to see what Jesus done in an action and reaction to everything. To be a Christian is to be Christ Like. It is not to be religious, it is not to look a certain way, it is not about money, race, if you are a male or female, or accolades. It is pure and it produces the fruits of the spirit and the gifts of the spirit as you draw near to Jesus Christ. The sole way to tell that you are a Christian is found only in your actions and reactions, hence the saying that I love, Show What You Know.

Do not let all the things that David, Moses, Daniel, Ester, Deborah, Samuel, Paul, Peter, John, and most importantly Jesus be taken for granted or in vain. They endured so much for you to know that you matter. They endured so much for you to know what to do in every situation. They paved the way for us to have an example of what it looks like to trust in God and go to God with action. They gave us the freedom we have now in the world and in Christ.

Now, you did not endure all the things you have endured to this day no matter what age you are or how little or big the endurance was for others or yourself not to grow and learn from it to be set free and saved. You have the Bible to go to, to confirm, to research, to access, to touch the hem of Jesus through. Many others do not. They do not have this access because they do not want to, and for some they have no opportunity to it.

They have been misled from the largest point of view that they are unworthy or the simplest point of view that they cannot read, understand, or remember what they read, so they do not even try. Both do not excuse them at all. However, it does not excuse you either. You are called. You are chosen. You are meant to come out from among the crowd and serve the Lord and His people. In your prayers, worship, salvation, and your deepest darkness humility moment when you surrendered, your heart said, "send me, I will go."

Therefore, once you get to know your family in Christ through the books of the entire bible. You will learn so much more about God, and yourself. You will also get to know about your family. You will

ENDURE

gain a wisdom and understanding that you are one with the Word of God, and God. You will download the Word of God into your Heart, Mind, and Motives by reading, studying, and applying it. Then you become that Word of God to others. I am not saying you are the Bible, God, Jesus or the Holy Spirit therefore do not start acting like you are in control. I am saying you become the evidence of the Bible. You become the proof of the promises. People begin to read the Word of God by reading you. In 1 Corinthians 6:9-20 God teaches us that Jesus walks the earth through you. No one knows this unless you allow Jesus, not the devil to shine through you.

1 Corinthians 6:9-11 Amplified Bible [9] Do you not know that the unrighteous will not inherit or have any share in the kingdom of God? Do not be deceived; [d] neither the sexually immoral, nor idolaters, nor adulterers, nor effeminate [by perversion], nor [e] those who participate in homosexuality, [10] nor thieves, nor the greedy, nor drunkards, nor revilers [whose words are used as weapons to abuse, insult, humiliate, intimidate, or slander], nor swindlers will inherit or have any share in the kingdom of God. [11] And such were some of you [before you believed]. But you were washed [by the atoning sacrifice of Christ], you were sanctified [set apart for God, and made holy], you were justified [declared free of guilt] in the name of the Lord

Jesus Christ and in the [Holy] Spirit of our God [the source of the believer's new life and changed behavior].

A renewing of the mind, body, image and heart changes. You will not remain the same. Make no mistake you can not say, " I will get myself together then come to Christ. You come to Him, knowing you need Him, and need change with an open heart, mind, eyes, ears and hands to receive Him and follow Him. He will send the Holy Spirit to teach you, guide you and remind you.

Therefore, do not say I do not read the bible because I do not understand it, or can not remember what I read. Just read it. The Holy Spirit knows His job, you need to learn and obeys yours.

John 14:26 Amplified But the Helper (Comforter, Advocate, Intercessor—Counselor, Strengthener, Standby), the Holy Spirit, whom the Father will send in My name [in My place, to represent Me and act on My behalf], He will teach you all things. And He will help you remember everything that I have told you.

It is important to remember that the Lord your God knows His job and how to do it. It is important for us to know our position.

ENDURE

1 Corinthians 6:12-20 Amplified Bible The Body Is the Lord's *¹²Everything is permissible for me, but not all things are beneficial. Everything is permissible for me, but I will not be enslaved by anything [and brought under its power, allowing it to control me]. ¹³Food is for the stomach and the stomach for food, but God will do away with both of them. The body is not intended for sexual immorality, but for the Lord, and the Lord is for the body [to save, sanctify, and raise it again because of the sacrifice of the cross]. ¹⁴And God has not only raised the Lord [to life], but will also raise us up by His power. ¹⁵Do you not know that your bodies are members of Christ? Am I therefore to take the members of Christ and make them part of a [l]prostitute? Certainly not! ¹⁶Do you not know that the one who joins himself to a prostitute is one body with her? For He says, "THE TWO SHALL BE ONE FLESH." ¹⁷But the one who is united and joined to the Lord is one spirit with Him. ¹⁸Run away from sexual immorality [in any form, whether thought or behavior, whether visual or written]. Every other sin that a man commits is outside the body, but the one who is sexually immoral sins against his own body. ¹⁹Do you not know that your body is a temple of the Holy Spirit who is within you, whom you have [received as a gift] from God, and that you are not your own [property]? [20] You were bought with a price [you were actually purchased with the precious blood of Jesus and made His own]. So then, honor and glorify God with your body.*

When you begin to come from among the tradition of family, friends, churches, religions there will be a rise. This rise will not be one of God, but it will definitely awaken many because you decided to come from among them and lead them in the way, the truth, and the life of Jesus. They will have no choice but to see their own ways, truths, and lives that they are now comfortable with. You must decide that you are ready. Being ready takes endurance to work for the Lord and to be of the Lord. It is not just a title, rank, or free ticket. It all comes with endurance. But this endurance brings forth so much joy and freedom.

Take an inventory on what you do that leads others to Christ. Ask God for wisdom, and understanding how to be the living Word of God among people. The very example of the Love of God. Once you get to know Jesus, you will be aware of what Jesus would or would not do. Then you will have a conviction upon you when you do things that Jesus would not do. This is not to condemn you, this is to allow you to have these things revealed and healed not only for you, but for those that witness the transformation in Christ. Decide to be that honorable man or women of God, that leads by the example of Christ not your standard traditions.

ENDURE

CHAPTER 5

Consider It Joy

James 1:2-4 Amplified Bible [2] Consider it nothing but joy, my [a] brothers and sisters, whenever you fall into various trials. [3] Be assured that the testing of your faith [through experience] produces endurance [leading to spiritual maturity, and inner peace]. [4] And let endurance have its perfect result and do a thorough work, so that you may be perfect and completely developed [in your faith], lacking in nothing.

After reading this verse, wow I do think I need to say one thing more. But of course, I will because God gives me loads to share. When I would first hear verses like this, especially when I was going through some really hard times, it was very hard to comprehend joy. I did not know what joy was let alone how to have it. Now I can say I do know what joy is and have it. The answer was within the verse, I just did not want to hear it, receive it, or have it. I wanted my way, and I wanted the hurt to just stop. The truth is if I had gotten my way, I would have never received joy from all the endurance I was suffering in and through. The first step of noticing you have faith as small as a mustard seed is your speech. You speak faith without even knowing it when others are praying for you and sowing into you. People you probably will never meet or know about. You say things like, " I am going through this." Did you see it, did you receive it? Did you notice the faith in that statement? I am going <u>through</u> this! You spoke in faith that you were not stuck in this, you said I am going through this. That is faith, and that is powerful. Hold on to that little faith, and then watch it unfold from faith-to-faith hereafter! It is coming.

You need the experience of the bully, not to become that bully. You need the experience of needing God to provide, so that you understand He is your provider. You need to know He is your Savior, Protector, Healer, Comforter because otherwise you will think you are, or that others are. Much like many do today. They will rush to the cops, doctor, parents, spouse, self-worth, boss, child, friend, socials, or their own ability before Christ.

To seek Christ first for a line of cars to move, or to find the keys, or to pay something outside of their budget is beyond their comprehension because they have been molded and trained that the people, places, and things of the world can only do that. When the truth is, they can only do it through Christ Jesus. The truth is they can only do what they are capable of. The truth is they have limitations, expectations, and judgement with all that they do. When Jesus says I can, I will, I have, but why can't you trust in me.

Romans 1:25 Amplified Bible, ²⁵ Because they exchanged the truth of God for a lie and worshiped and served the creature rather than the Creator, Who is blessed forever! Amen (so be it).

So be it, wow! God says if you are your own god, so be it. If they are greater than me, to you, so be it. If you do not trust me, so be it. This means you do not believe in me, so, so be it! We must learn how foolish it is when we trust a creature, or creation over the Creator.

We are trained early on to trust in people, places, and things in the world, by parents, and so many more. It is our natural way of thinking, so to think in the supernatural is beyond our comprehension until one day it is not. Joy is being content in the matter; it runs a close race with peace and patience and works in conjunction with them. You will hear of something that normally would shake you, and then suddenly one day due to the endurance, the faith system, and the bond you are creating with God, you become Joy Filled, knowing He got it, and you got Him to go to.

Jesus is teaching us that when perseverance comes, count it joy because that means something huge between, and with Him is coming. Something so grand that joy will be born in it, and you will have abundance. The devil knows this, so he tries his very best to get all up in your ear and say, " what are you going to do now, how are you going to get through this, what if they say this about you, you look so weak, you need to do this to get that." Does this sound familiar? If it does, this means you are not in the Word of God enough.

    Jesus teaches us we hear and do what we put into our bodies. Therefore, if you are putting in the Word of God, then the Word of God will be heard and done over the word of the enemy. It is an easy fix. Go get in the Word of God. You cannot fight battles of the spirit without your sword of the spirit and your shield of faith. You will not hear the Lord is my Shepard I shall not want, over what are you going to do or who are you going to ask. If you are not in your Word of God, it is harder to hear God. Think about it. How will you know God's word, or voice. How will you know what God would say to you, if you do not know His word. It is that simple. You know the word of the devil, because you are hearing it in songs, shows, conversations, and more. You choose to hear and feed the flesh over the spirit. This is the truth, so that the truth can set you free. We need the truth.

    Hold your peace and keep your eyes fixed on the Lord. He is the Lion and the Lamb; He knows what He needs to do. He knows what to do. He is waiting to see if you will activate Him in faith! Or if you will say, " I got it". You cannot do this Lord it is too big for you." Did you know that is what you say to Him when you do things without Him?

Take an inventory of what you trust in the Lord for and what you do not. Have you just gotten through a huge financial, medical, marriage, family matter with tremendous faith knowing with every part of your body, mind, heart, and soul that He could heal, provide, protect and saw because of that faith that He did it. Then you receive that random text, call, mail, or visit from somone or something so much smaller and random and then freak out as if you have no faith at all? Kind of weird right? It is not weird to God. It is on purpose. You see he has mercy and grace for us on the deepest levels of love. Therefore, He knows that He must show some of us the massive things He can and will do, so that we can begin to trust Him with the little that we think we can do on our own. It is all a healing process. It is not a lack of faith. He reveals to heal. You must decide to use the revealing for healing, not an attack or a setback.

ENDURE

CHAPTER 6

Be The Image Of Christ

Hebrews 12:1-2 Amplified Bible Jesus, the Example 12 Therefore, since we are surrounded by so great a cloud of [a] witnesses [who by faith have testified to the truth of God's absolute faithfulness], stripping off every unnecessary weight and the sin which so easily and cleverly entangles us, let us run with endurance and active persistence the race that is set before us, 2 [looking away from all that will distract us and] focusing our eyes on Jesus, who is the Author and Perfecter of faith [the first incentive for our belief and the One who brings our faith to maturity], who for the joy [of accomplishing the goal] set before Him endured the cross, [b]disregarding the shame, and sat down at the right hand of the throne of God [revealing His deity, His authority, and the completion of His work].

You ever woke up and just felt like, oh my, I have allot to do

ENDURE

today, you literally felt the weight of the list, the day, the title, responsibility, and your body physically & spiritually on you? Often the things we carry spiritually feel like such a weight because we are not properly distributing it to Christ. Sure, we pray before we get up and believe with an action by getting up, but that weight is still there. Why? When it comes to a day-to-day task, thought, or challenge we have difficulty immediately casting our cares on the Lord. Do you wonder why? Do you wonder if this is lack of faith?

Recently while enduring the recovery of my fourth brain surgery that I have had in the past one and a half years; I had hoped and still have hope that it was the final one needed. You see, I am believing God will keep the remaining veins in my neck and brain wide open and not allow them to narrow or kink anymore. With the first three suregeries, almost immediately, I felt better, and those surgeries seemed much more intense than the last one I endured, although it was not. The last one was longer and this time they put a stent in my brain to keep the veins open more and to allow the blood to flow better and decrease the fluid that continues to want to form in my spine and brain causing extreme pressure in my head, especially in my left eye and ear. When I awoke from the suregy I was thinking wow, I will be told some grand news and go home. Instead, I was told we opened all the veins in your entire brain with a balloon. We will do scans and see how it looks around 3am to see if we need to go back in due to your jugular veins they were severely narrow, nearly being completely closed. They asked me if anyone had ever choked me. No one ever physically choked me, but I could take a good guess on who was spiritually trying to choke me and take me out.

The doctor went on to say how he did not like to put a stent up and down it is too risky it could move, and if it did it would go to my heart. In addition, the way my jawbone is the doctor said he cannot get to my jugular vein so someone would have to modify my jawbone to get there. Of course, then I would deal with the pains and changes of that in my jaw, speech, eating, and otherwise. I know the power of the jawbone that Jesus taught us with Jacob therefore I know my God can move what He needs to move and heal what he needs to heal. I also know my faith has to be in line with Him on this one because he is reaching many others with my testimony. That type of faith does not come easy. But it is possible.

When approached with this news, I felt the audience, the demon warriors, the angels of the devil. The devil brought out the entire pack to celebrate. They were ready to cheer together and charge at me all at the same time. They wanted to make sure I was down and defeated. I could almost see them, I felt them so boldly. The weight began to overload me, the anger, the pain, the why, the what now began to try to consume me. It was like a spirit army with full weapons charging towards me. All I could shout was NO, get the behind me satan. You are not coming around this mind nor this bed! You do not have authority over my mind, nor my brain. You have no authority over my life, my future, my circumstances, my family, these doctors or otherwise. Nothing of mine is yours get away from me now. I immediately felt and saw the Angels of the Lord, and the Angel Army the Lord had encamped all around me, the room was full and surrounded and so was the situation. God was there and so were they. He says He encamps them ready for us, but we are the Sargent of our lives. We must call them to action. Why? He wants to know if we trust in Him or the devil. We must learn to call on Him first.

The book of James teaches us in Chapter 2 faith without works is dead. We have been seeing faith without works is dead from Genesis to Revelations through our brothers and sisters in Christ in the word of God. It is not only a love letter packed with our access. The Word of God is a road map to Heaven. The Word of God is also filled with Hope, and how to access our promises with an action. When you get to know Abraham, Job, Joseph, Esther, Deborah, Daniel, King Saul, Jonah, Mary the Mother of Jesus, and most of all Jesus you will see faith activated. That is one of the reasons it is so important to read your bible. You are given the way, the truth, and the life. It is your owner's manual.

When you in the fire and you feel things are so hot, that there is no way out other than Jesus you will think about Shadrach,

Meshach, and Abednego and you will know Jesus is in that fire with you. You will know you will come out of that furnace (situation) and you will not even have your clothes singed or smell of that fire. Our brothers Shadrach, Meshach, and Abednego got in the fiery furnace literally. Why? To reveal to us when we would be addressed with the fire spiritually, we would know Jesus can, allowing Jesus to be your first go to. It is best to always keep Him with you, because we need Him. Unlike our brothers Shadrach, Meshach, and Abednego we often do not physically go through a fire that can burn us. But it does not make the flame, the heat, or the pain feel any less painful for a long time.

    Just like when someone is burned physically, we must go through care while waiting for the skin (flesh) to heal or get new flesh put on it. Are you receiving this? Jesus is saying, "I will keep you from even being burned, but if you do get burned. I am right here then too. I will not leave you or forsake you." I will take care of the flesh and renew your spirit.

    Each individual matter no matter how big or how small it is allows us to be baptized by fire. The Holy Spirit fire. It molds us to be transformed. The Lord wants us to only look back, if we are looking back to be that witness or to witness from faith to faith. The Lord teaches us to stop looking back to failures, and the people, places, and things He has taken us from. He showed us that with our brother and sister, Lot and his wife. When he looked ahead he was saved and was the salt (example of Christ), when she looked back, she turned to salt and not the kind used to flavor the world that Jesus speaks of in Matthew 5:13-16. She turned to a pillar of salt that remained and melted to nothing.

    Meet your brothers and sisters in Christ and take the time to speak with your family about their memories, and faith. This will all be the crowd of witness you need to live from faith to faith. You have a huge crowd of witnesses looking at you, especially if are known to mess up things allot in life with loss, addiction, finances or otherwise. So why not use that huge platform of witness that the enemy wants to shame you with. Use it for the good of God so others can see how powerful Jesus is. Show them Jesus. You are packing the King of Kings in you.

    Yes, it is hard. I know. The symptoms I endure daily while waiting on the Lord to heal me is hard, painful, and feels like a heavy weight. But I know how hard it had to be for Abraham to wait years to have a son, then have to walk that son to the altar to be sacrificed. I know how hard it had to be for Shadrach, Meshach, and Abednego to stand against all the people of the entire town and say no I will not worship you I rather get in the fire. I also know how hard it had to be for Jonah when he realized "I messed up" now I am in the belly of a huge fish and deep down in the sea. It took faith. It took believing in

Jesus Christ to be rescued, provided for, protected. When you decide to believe with action (works) your whole life transforms. Stop believing that you can protect, provide, and rescue yourself, or others can do more than God. You may never admit that with a word, but what does your actions say?

    Wake up knowing you in a race to the finish line with Jesus every day. You are never in competition with others, never! They will never be you, and you will never be them. You must decide that the race is to be better than you were yesterday, and you will always win. This will become a natural being to you, but not at first. You know that you must study to learn more things. You know you must train to do bigger, better things. You know you must exercise to get to the goals you have. That all takes endurance. It is uncomfortable, it is hard, it hurts but once you reach the goal it is victorious. Why? Because you achieved what you wanted to achieve. If you are not trying to achieve a closer life with Christ it shows. If you are not trying to train for His access, then that shows. You must decide or ask why this does not matter as much as the worldly things. Once you get to know you, then you will know how to get to know Christ.

    What would motivate you to train, study, exercise? Is Jesus not more than that to you? Is your eternal life not more valuable to you. As you draw to Christ in your training and run that race towards Him. Others will see you. You have a big crowd of witnesses ready to see

ENDURE

you win, or lose. Use that platform to show people Christ in you. Not from knowledge. That is the easy part. Let them meet Him and see their access to Him, through your endurance for Him while trusting in Him.

Remember you can take that weight off and hand it to Jesus. He says I will take it, you just got to give it to me. Choose to believe Him over yourself, the doctors, the boss, the enemies, and the supporters. Let your life reflect that Jesus is in you, not just on your shirt or coming out of your mouth.

Take an inventory on what or who you go to when you lost your keys. Does it look like, 'WHERE IS MY KEYS, I AM GOING TO BE SO LATE, WHO DID NOT PUT MY KEYS BACK" does this sound like Jesus? Have you arrived to say, Lord remind me where I put my kids or who had my keys last, then remind them before I get to them where they put them. I can assure you, that you will freak out your kids/spouse/parents/friends with this new reaction. You will show Jesus, even in this you seeked Him first. Lastly you will find your keys much sooner by asking Him, instead of the alternative.

Take the time to take an inventory on what you do when things appear to be a setback, attack, distraction, temptation. Not just bad things. Cute grandbabies, outings with friends, and that juicy burger when you know you having issues can be those things too. Do you look to it as an opportunity to Show What You Know or do you go straight to, the devil is attacking or tempting me? Stop giving him attention. The devil is not your father. Think of your brother Job then ask, what is this really about. Will this lead me to Christ or away from Him. Will this lead me to the plans God has for me or will this lead me away from them.

CHAPTER 7

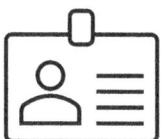

Your Identity

Romans 5:3-4 Amplified Bible 3 And not only this, but [with joy] let us exult in our sufferings and rejoice in our hardships, knowing that hardship (distress, pressure, trouble) produces patient endurance; 4 and endurance, proven character (spiritual maturity) ; and proven character, hope and confident assurance [of eternal salvation].

I did not receive this until I finally received this! It is from the toe that gets hit and you finally do not shout with anger. It is the loss you endure of money or things, and you feel settled in peace knowing it is okay. It is the report about your health, and you sit there with assurance that God is the Healer. This may come to some right away without the endurance, but not for me. I had to endure it, I had to go through it, and within it all this scripture is true, you produce your true new character, confidence, and access to your salvation.

Many say well salvation is free. Yes, you right it sure is. Thank you Jesus. But I can assure you if I purchase you a burger or a bible and give it to you freely, and you choose not to pick it up and eat it or read it; what do you have? You need to taste of it, you need the access of it, you need to eat (receive) it and let it have its way with you. I can assure you that when you repent, that is day one, that is not sealing the deal.

    You will absolutely not be protected to go to heaven from that one act of repentance especially if you did not mean it or remember it. Jesus Christ came and served, and showed us the way, the truth, and the life. Jesus showed us all things so we could live a life that is by example of Him. He shows us this throughout the gospels in the books of Matthew, Mark, Luke, and John as well as from Genesis to Revelations. You are no different from Moses, Noah, or anyone else because of your family status or your circumstances. You do get the free pass, but that looks like humbly asking for forgiveness of your sins and deciding to learn and get to know Jesus. By doing this you will transform by the renewing of your mind, mouth, and motives. In doing this you will begin to walk from faith to faith. That comes with endurance that you begin to witness. It is not temptation; it is not an attack.

    Endurance filters the bad, the ugly, the pain, the hurt, the pride out of you. It is the filtration system you need. It is like a dialyses machine for kidneys. You hook up to Jesus and He is going to clean out your blood line, and renew your strength to walk in the way, the truth, and the life. His word teaches us that it is impossible to please God without faith. In Matthew 7:15-21 the word of God teaches us that unless we produce the fruits of the spirit we are not of God. You must know the truth so the truth can set you free.

Hebrews 11:6 Amplified Bible ⁶ But without faith it is impossible to [walk with God and] please Him, for whoever comes [near] to God must [necessarily] believe that God exists and that He rewards those who [earnestly and diligently] seek Him.

Matthew 7:15-21 Amplified Bible A Tree and Its Fruit ¹⁵ "Beware of the false prophets, [teachers] who come to you dressed as sheep [appearing gentle and innocent], but inwardly are ravenous wolves. ¹⁶ By their fruit you will recognize them [that is, by their contrived doctrine and self-focus]. Do people pick grapes from thorn bushes or figs from thistles? ¹⁷ Even so, every healthy tree bears good fruit, but the unhealthy tree bears bad fruit. ¹⁸ A good tree cannot bear bad fruit, nor can a bad tree bear good fruit. ¹⁹ Every tree that does not bear good fruit is cut down and thrown into the fire. ²⁰ Therefore, by their fruit you will recognize them [as false prophets]. ²¹ "Not everyone who says to Me, 'Lord, Lord,' will enter the kingdom of heaven, but only he who does the will of My Father who is in heaven.

Too many know the word, go to church, and sacrifice so much and they never fall in love with Jesus, or they lose their love for Jesus. In Revelation 2, Jesus says that there is one thing He will hold against us if we do not love Him. He goes into great detail how the church (we) lose our love for Him. He also goes into great detail that we will not go to heaven because of that. Whether we assume we saved or not.

We need God's checkups. We tend to have no issue with doctor exams, testing for college, or testing to see what we have at the hospital or have done. But we are not taught enough that the distractions, temptations, loss, setbacks, rejection is those exams to determine your new reaction. Yes, they may be terrible for doing what they have done to you. Yes, the situation may be terrible. No one is denying that. But what is your reaction to that, is it faith? If not, why? Endurance and perseverance are needed. It truly develops the fruits of the spirit within you.

When I first read about this in the word of God through James, Revelations, Matthew, Hebrews and more, I felt so convicted.

ENDURE

Like Jesus just said *NOW*, sit down and listen. I did not say to do that, I did not ask you for that, do you not know to be still I am God! We cannot lose heart in the why. We cannot get caught up in how many we are baptizing, helping, or giving to. We cannot get caught up in attendance and serving then not have a relationship with the Lord. You can easily become your own god that way, or the god of others. You must discern what you are doing and why you are doing it daily.

You will know that you are healing, delivered, and sanctified when that person that you been helping rejects you, and you feel peace. When somthing does not go your way and you feel self-control. When someone comes against you, and you feel mercy and grace. When someone is in need of a conversation or your time and you feel kindness, and goodness. When you are told something that would normally bring your fear and you have faith activated instead. When the normal would be to hate and instead you choose to love.

Ask yourself what is my reaction? How long have I been a Christian and am I transforming or still going around and around the same way. What comes out of me most, hate or love? Jesus teaches us to love Him and others with all your heart, all your mind, and all your soul. Hearing this may make you think of that person, you know you do not love, and feel some sort of way about it. You may be thinking He does not want me around this person, they hurt me bad. Guess what you are right! He did not say you will stay around them, like or love their ways. He says you are to love them. Love is not the feel good I cannot wait to hold you love He is speaking of. Love is found in 1 Corinthians.

1 Corinthians 13:4-8 Amplified Bible *⁴Love endures with patience and serenity, love is kind and thoughtful, and is not jealous or envious; love does not brag and is not proud or arrogant. ⁵It is not rude; it is not self-seeking, it is not provoked [nor overly sensitive and easily angered]; it does not take into account a wrong endured. ⁶It does not rejoice at injustice, but rejoices with the truth [when right and truth prevail]. ⁷Love bears all things [regardless of what comes], believes all things [looking for the best in each one], hopes all things [remaining steadfast during difficult times], endures all things [without weakening]. ⁸Love never fails [it never fades nor ends]. But as for prophecies, they will pass away; as for tongues, they will cease; as for the gift of special knowledge, it will pass away.*

Turns out you do love them, right? Because you are always tolerating and enduring them. Somehow someway you give chances, you still pray for them, and you do not provoke them or boast about yourself. And if you do, you now know how love by not doing that any longer, right? Now you know what love is and how much God has changed you and me, so we can agree if He can transform us, their chances are not bad, amen? He is able. He did not say they need to be able. Jesus Christ is able, so when we stop complaining, fearing, defending then Jesus will step in and remove them, shut the mouth of the lion, give you the sling shot, or show you how mighty He is in their healing. You do your part, let *"Him and them"* do their part.

That is when you are showing Jesus your love for Him in an action. That is when you know you love Him. How do I know this? When Peter refused Jesus three times before He was crucified Jesus then came back to Peter after the resurrection. You will notice Peter also went back to the first place He met Jesus, that is where Jesus came to him. Jesus asked Peter 3 times if he loved Him, and Peter said you know I love you. But Jesus kept on asking Peter, and telling Peter then feed and take care of my sheep and lambs then. In translation that means if you Love me Peter, then go tell people about me with action and intent. Do not lose your love for me in doing it. Feed them by showing them Me in you. Take care of them by showing them who I am and what I would do. He was not just meaning to serve them by giving them food and taking care of them. He meant if you love Me Peter, get up and show me.

Take an inventory of who knows you are of God from your actions and reactions through faith. The people at church may know, but do the people at home, work, school know? Do you represent Jesus when something does not go your way, are you allowing the horrible things you have endured, and still endure to glorify the devil and distract others from God? Does your endurance produce joy yet? Fear not, Joy is coming!

CHAPTER 8

Focus On The Race

James 1:12 Amplified Bible 12 Blessed [happy, spiritually prosperous, favored by God] is the man who is steadfast under trial and perseveres when tempted; for when he has passed the test and been approved, he will receive the [victor's] crown of life which the Lord has promised to those who love Him.

To be steadfast is simply to put one foot in front of the other day by day, and moment by moment. Do not look to the ones that appear to be running the marathon and blessed in your sight. Do not look down on the ones you feel are less than or beneath your growth in the world or in the spirit. You only know what you see. To be honest God only shows you their growth and failures to give you hope, assignments, and to give you healing. You can look at a person doing less than you and discern, not judge that you are growing. That you are no longer in that state, or that you could have been in that state without His covering of mercy and grace. This is important to know with wisdom and understanding. It keeps you from judgement me of others and ultimately being judged by God. It keep you with hope and humble as well.

Decide to do your part and pray scriptures over anyone that you are concerned about. To pray with purpose is to pray with faith and not feelings. Oh, you know the prayers I am speaking of the ones that say, Lord help them to get up and clean their house, they are so lazy and nasty. Instead activate Psalms 23:1, the verse someone else prayed over you possibly, to help you out of your pit. Say, Lord you are their Shepard they shall not want in Jesus' name amen. Sound better? Trust me it works better too. Use what worked on you, for them. That is using your endurance for the good of others. To be able to reflect on your short comings or needs that you are now done with and say, I know God can, because He did this for me.

Then there is the oh, Lord help them to not take all that medication, take their access away. Do not pray like that. You will cause way more harm than good. If God takes away the medication, the access, the options but not the source (pain and addiction) then you just caused a bigger mess. Instead activate the word of God in faith by saying, oh Lord you are their healer, heal them and let them be healed, saved them and let them be saved for you are the one we

ENDURE

praise in Jesus' name amen. You find this in Jeremiah 17:14! Use the evidence you have from your endurance. Your reaction now shows the Lord appreciation, honor, and integrity. Your faith gives you the knowledge that you have been set free and you know that it can set others free too. Learn how to pray in faith. That will work much better.

Have you ever said oh, Lord help them to clean themselves up better or get off the street and get a job? Instead activate the word of God, say "Lord you are their provider, protector, counselor, prince of peace, Lord save them in Jesus name amen." I am telling you that this works better. When you call things out as you see them, that is showing either your lack of faith or your growth in faith. What are you seeing? Do you have eyes to see, and ears to hear spiritually or do you look at the plain vision of the world and see the addict, the hurt, the dying, the financial issues, the fear? Ask God to help you hear and see Him and His ways over the ways of the world.

Do you catch yourself saying oh, Lord help them to not be so prideful and angry so that others can tolerate them. Oh, really!! Or how does Jesus say it? Oh, you of little faith! Your job is to see and pray. Your job is to be Christ like in the reaction to them. Your job is to look at them and be greatful you not them, or that you are not them any longer. Sometimes we encounter pride filled angry people before we get a position of leadership or growth of any kind. Even growth as a parent, friend, spouse, co-worker. Leaders are not just bosses, pastors and presidents. God will allow that person around you, and show you what it is like to be treated that way for the following reasons:

1. To know what it feels like, not to become them in the title, or position He is about to give you.

2. To you to utilize the word of God and show what you know.

3. To intercede in prayer with wonder why are they so pride filled or angry to pray for the source of it to be healed because they do not know how, and there is no one else but you.

I pray this helps enlighten the ways the Lord sees things. He tells us His ways are not our ways. Once we get to know Him, we get to see His ways much more clearly. We begin to see we are never under attack. We are just in the exam room but with Him the Teacher is always present to guide, teach, and remind. It is always an open book test spiritually and literally.

The next time you see someone overworking in your view,

do not pray for them to be still or have time off. Pray for God to be their provider. You do not know why they are hustling. You do not need to know. All you need to know it that you need to ask God to provide for their needs and bless them with wisdom and understanding. God will handle the rest. He gets that you care for them. He understands you discern that they need rest in your opinion. But it is up to God and them on what to do next. Help them by praying scripture, not feelings.

When you are concerned when somone does not show up, or want to be around family gatherings, church, or take care of their responsibilities. Pray for favor over them, pray that God will give them wisdom and understanding with a sound mind of power, love and authority in Christ Jesus. Use your scriptures that is what they are they're for. Our feeling come from our views and opinions. Our faith comes from our soul and spirit. Allow your soul and spirit to always override your flesh. When you start to pray in faith with scripture that pray not only activates for those you prayed for. God goes deep down into your heart and begins to answer, heal, and bless you with your deepest hearts desires.

When you see someone with a life, circumstance, or even a yard that is a mess, decide what you want and can do about it. Stop sharing your feeling about it, stop complaining about it, stop fearing it.

Decide you are enduring this to be the mighty prayer warrior or servant God has called you to be. Do not assume they do not have it together, they lazy, or they do not care. Many people do not help others, they prefer to talk about others instead. Many are working and hurting so badly that they cannot take care of the things that you were gifted to take care of. Maybe you noticed their issue because God is calling you to help them because you do have the time, money and strength that they do not have at this moment.

Many would rather spend three hours talking about someone's yard, life, or circumstances and how lazy they are than to spend one hour helping them clean it up for money or free. You not being paid to gossip for the three hours but you sure will do that. So why not get out there and spend that time sowing in prayer or labor for free, and be blessed by them or God for doing it. You honestly do not know if they can pay well or not just by the appearance. Be like Christ, do not be like the devil.

God knew you could not endure what they can and do endure. God also knows that they cannot endure what you have and do endure. God has a plan for everyone not to be without. Everyone! We must decide to look to Him and receive that access. Know that when that person in desperate need decides to set their eyes on the Lord, that you will see a grand transformation!

ENDURE

God knows our hearts, minds, souls, and abilities. He even knows who will be bad forever or not. Do not assume someone that you see as evil should go through something that your family, friend, neighbor is going through instead. You know what I am talking about, right? *"Why do they have to endure that they are so kind, loving, young, hardworking? While this one is a murderer, thief, cheater, rapist, and destroying people why does this not happen to them if it needs to happen?"* How do you know they both are not destroying people? We must learn God has a plan. He is not going to let someone endure something for no reason at all. He is trying to reach people through it, not just the person enduring it.

We must discern in love we have the power to change the world. God says we have the power in our tongue and in our faith. He also teaches this in the book of James. You have to decide to use endurance for perseverance not a good ole pity party, or to boast about yourself as if you are better than them. When you see something in your view that you want to have that others have. Do not take it as bait of distraction or temptation. Take it as a clue, or a puzzle piece to the master plan God has for you. Let it be the thing that allows you to notice, hey I want to strive for that too. Lord is that for me, or is it a distraction, do not fear asking Him this.

Most do not want to ask because they do not want the answer. They want it, they like the color of it, and they do not know why that bad person got it before them. That is none of your business. Our business is the plans God has for us. He says ask and we will receive if we believe and if we do not ask with the wrong motives. Check out James 4. You see we love the picture, and the promise that if you ask you will receive it if you believe. But we do not like the verse that says if you ask with the wrong motives, you will not receive it.

Maybe you do not need it at all or not right now because it will distract you from God, then you are better off without it. Like that baby, friend, job, or spouse that you begged the Lord for, then you put that person, place, or thing before Him. He says it is better to not have it at all than to lose your soul over it. So, guess what? If you can activate self-control, a fruit you already have, then you can get it. Because you will not put it before God.

James 4:2-3 Amplified Bible ² *You are jealous and covet [what others have] and [a]your lust goes unfulfilled; so you [b]murder. You are envious and cannot obtain [the object of your envy]; so you fight and battle. You do not have because you do not ask [it of God].* ³ *You ask [God for something] and do not receive it, because you ask [c]with wrong motives [out of selfishness or with an unrighteous agenda], so that [when you get what you want] you may spend it on your [hedonistic] desires.*

ENDURE

Take an inventory of what you have asked for that you put before God. Take an inventory on that person, place, or thing that you been asking for and ask God to not allow you to put it before Him, to give you wisdom and understanding with it. Watch how things change for you.

Take an inventory on the plans you make for others when you see their home, body, options, and more. Do you say things like, if I were them I would do this and that or do you pray for them?

CHAPTER 9

Do Not Give Up

Philippians 3:13-14 Amplified Bible [13] [a] *Brothers and sisters, I do not consider that I have made it my own yet; but one thing I do: forgetting what lies behind and reaching forward to what lies ahead,* [14] *I press on toward the goal to win the [heavenly] prize of the upward call of God in Christ Jesus.*

We can not forget what we are doing everything for. We are doing everything for our love for the Lord. When we attend, give, serve, help, live all of it can become very overwhelming especially if the enemy tries to tempt you with competition, or a goal. You can get so caught up in what you want or do not have that you will forget what the main part of your bond with Jesus is, to fall in love with Him. To build a relationship with Him, and to build a foundation on Him. Do not lose sight of that.

Your time in church is not your time alone with the Lord. Time serving, attending, or reading the word of God is not going to give you a star or check mark in the Book of Lambs. Those are natural abilities you start to do in the spirit as you become in a close relationship with the Lord. Those works should not feel like a chore list, or a honey do list. They should feel like peace. If peace is not in it, if eagerness and joy is not in it, then the Lord is not in it. So, am I saying do not do it, if you do not feel like it? No, at first you will have to go through the endurance of training just like we spoke of in the prior chapters.

When you first start to learn that new language it is hard. When you first start to exercise it is hard. When you first start to eat better it is hard. When you begin to study for exams and take on new challenges it is hard. You do it because you want and desire to see the finished result for you to look better, feel better, achieve more, and access more in communication, right? You see the world has taught us this is natural so we follow along and strive. Why would we think learning, exercising, starting a new language, eating better or reaching higher positions with Christ is not worth the endurance then? We do not mind it for self, right?

It comes from this root that the enemy has tricked us with. Maybe you are the one overlooked, or disrespected because of the

ENDURE

love, mercy, grace, forgiveness you have for others. Maybe you are taken for granted like Jesus is because you will give chance after chance and wait because you see so much potential in them. Maybe you try to go out of your way like Jesus and forgive and help again. Or maybe you are the one that takes advantage of people like Jesus because you know He is always waiting, loving, giving, forgiving and has those arms wide open no matter what. If you are that person that forgives, loves, helps no matter what. You know the pain Jesus feels in this. You know that you are more like Christ than you think. If you are the person that takes people for granted like this, then you now know the reason you do it. You do it because you expect them to always be waiting to help, serve, love, forgive, fix it.

One day that person you take for granted will no longer be with you. Will you decide to be angry at God for taking away your god, or will you understand that person often must be set free because they done their part for the Lord, now the Lord needs to move them so that you will do your part and they will reap in heaven from theirs. Wisdom and understanding of endurance are hard to receive. It is real and it is raw. It is very direct and clear once you receive it. It is one of the gifts you will obtain as you grow in the fruit of long suffering. But it packs a fulfilled punch of clarity once you are sanctified and delivered in it.

If you have had that person in your life that you have regrets because you did not say goodbye, or you did not show you appreciated them; know that they have already forgiven you. That is their heart. They were not only doing it for you, but they were also serving God because they know you needed that type of love in your life. Do not look back to that regret just ask the Lord to forgive you and help you to let it go. You can honor that person by carrying on what they sowed in you and others. Use their endurance they had for you, and with you to allow others to have what they gave to you. That is how you truly say sorry, I appreciate you and goodbye.

The grand prize is always Jesus, and your access to Him. When running a race to get to the finish line we often do not get the reward until we make it there first. With Jesus, we receive Him at the starting line, and He runs side by side with you the entire time. When you get to that finish line you share the victory together, and all the angels in heaven cheer you on too.

You must discern that you truly not giving up anything that added to your life, you are breaking free from the bondage that held you back. You can look at "your thing" as chains that bind you like you were in prison. The enemy makes you feel like sin is freedom. He is crafty in that way. He makes you feel like great and horrible things must happen because you so bad or so good. But Jesus shows you the true way, truth, and life. He loved you so much that He not only died for you, but He also came and lived thirty-three years in the flesh for you. How do you think that made Him feel to know He had to leave in the flesh in thirty-three years. His mother, friends, family, disciples and the sinners. In Matthew 26-28 you will see how much pain and sorrow He was in. He was in such a great sorrow that He even asked God to take the cup if it was possible but if it was not He was ready to die for us. Through the book of Matthew, you will meet Jesus personally. You will see His birth, His connections to the disciples, friends, and family. You will see the joy, the peace, the promise, the protection, the rejection, the temptation from the devil, all of it. Why? He walked out every moment you would endure so that you would know He is not just telling you, He endured it too, for you. But because He endured it, He saved your life. Now you just have to decide that you want to do that for Him and for others that He trusts you with.

    We must make our normal, natural, and tradition centered on Jesus Christ and His Way, Truth and Life and stop making sure our children have the best shoes, clothes, titles, friends, times and make sure they know Jesus. If you truly love them, you will show this with an action. By interceding in conversations, faith, action, and serving. You show them what you know in action. You show them Jesus in you with that choice to change your reaction. If you do not do this with them, it is harder for them to acclimate to Jesus once they know about Him. It feels odd, awkward, and against natural tradition, and the world. You have a responsibility as a parent for the Lord just like Mary and Jospeh. Jesus teaches us this in 1 Corinthians to come from among the crowd and show the world that you are packing the King of Kings inside of you. That you are of Him. Because if you do not you will find out that you do not have a bond with Him at all and all that you have endured will be for nothing. Revelations 2 says so.

If you get to know Mary and Joseph you can find this in the beginning of Matthew, and Luke intimately. You will receive who they were and who God chose to raise His one and only son. You will no longer feel so defeated, unworthy and you will comprehend you raising His child so that His child can get back home. If you messed it all up until now, do not look back. Look ahead, what will you do now. Do not worry, God will use all that was bad for your good and the good of many others. You cannot change what happened now, but you can change what happens today, so decide to rise up and show what you know.

Take an inventory of what you need to do or do that introduces others to the Lord in your daily actions and reactions. No you do not have to pack the bible under your arm into school or the doctor's office. Download it in your heart, mind, and soul. What goes into the body comes out naturally right. If you eat food, mess comes out, right? So if you eat the word of God, by reading it and receiving it, then

ENDURE

the Messiah will come out.

CHAPTER 10

Finish The Race

1 Corinthians 9:24 Amplified Bible ^{24 [a]}*Do you not know that in a race all the runners run [their very best to win], but only one receives the prize? Run [your race] in such a way that you may seize the prize and make it yours!*

Keep your eyes on the Lord, know that He is both the Lion and the Lamb. He is the Lion of Judah the protector of all, and He is not about to allow no one, or nothing harm you. He is also a Father of honor and integrity and knows it takes correction and whippens to get you in line and allow you to grow from your mistakes and failures. He does stay close to you, but He is like a Lamb not a helicopter parent. He is not your reserve or your last resort. He is to be respected, honored and glorified. He is the perfect Man, the Perfect Father. He is so loving, and so merciful. You have no idea of the many things He protects you from as the Lion and the Lamb in your life. You just know of the things you speak to Him about only.

Revelation 5 Amplified Bible The Scroll with Seven Seals
5 I saw in the right hand of Him who was seated on the throne a scroll written on the inside and on the back, closed and sealed with seven seals. ² And I saw a strong angel announcing with a loud voice, "Who is worthy [having the authority and virtue] to open the scroll and to [a] break its seals?" ³ And no one in heaven or on earth or under the earth [in Hades, the realm of the dead] was able to open the scroll or look into it. ⁴ And I began to weep greatly because no one was found worthy to open the scroll or look into it. ⁵ Then one of the [twenty-four] elders said to me, "Stop weeping! Look closely, the Lion of the tribe of Judah, the Root of David, has overcome and conquered! He can open the scroll and [break] its seven seals."

This verse should confirm to you that no one or nothing has the power over you but the Lord. No one can determine one thing in your life. You can choose to follow temptation, but when you do that is your choice and the things you reap from it are also your choice. The things you reap to your generation is your choice. Here God is reminding you only He can complete this mission, and you can only be with Him at the finish line if you have decided to follow Him. Follow Him like you are looking up to the Lion of Judah. Knowing He is there watching you to protect you, guide you, and teach you. Know that He wants you to get home safely. But just like any cub that decides to stray, know that He still sees you and is watching over you. He is waiting and hoping that you would just come back home because you miss Him, love Him, and know that you need Him.

Revelation 14 Amplified Bible The Lamb and the 144,000 on Mount Zion **14** *Then I looked, and this is what I saw: the Lamb stood [firmly established] on Mount Zion, and with Him a hundred and forty-four thousand who had His name and His Father's name inscribed on their foreheads [signifying God's own possession].* *² And I heard a voice from heaven, like the sound of great waters and like the rumbling of mighty thunder; and the voice that I heard [seemed like music and] was like the sound of harpists playing on their harps.* *³ And they sang a new song before the throne [of God] and before the four living creatures and the elders; and no one could learn the song except the hundred and forty-four thousand who had been purchased (ransomed, redeemed) from the earth.* *⁴ These are the ones who have not been defiled [by relations] with women, for they are celibate. These are the ones who follow the Lamb wherever He goes.*

ENDURE

These have been purchased and redeemed from among men [of Israel] as the first fruits [sanctified and set apart for special service] for God and the Lamb. ⁵ No lie was found in their mouth, for they are blameless (spotless, untainted, beyond reproach).

God knows you going through it, but as the Lion and the Lamb you can always look to that mountain top and see both are there for you. God knows your heart, your plans, your future, your abilities, and your weaknesses. He is accepting you with open arms and wanting to teach you that at all times, in all ways just look up. Look up knowing He is there for you. Look up knowing He will rescue you. Look up with faith knowing you will be with Him. He wants nothing more than to tell you, "Well done my good and faithful child." He wants you to hear the one thing you been needing to hear.

Most of the things you do is to hear "well done" from others whether you know it or not. You want to know if you are doing enough or doing well. Because of this you put many expectations on yourself and others or you do not have expectations at all. Jesus Christ is the Author and Finisher. Jesus Christ is the Creator not the creature or the creation. He can do more than anyone, any place, or anything. You just have to decide in your mind, heart, soul, and actions that He can. When you do, things change, you transform, and you draw others to Christ.

The Lion is ready and setting on that mountain top so bold and so calm. He is the most confident because He knows that not one person can defeat Him. The Lamb is gentle and loving and has so much self-control, grace, kindness, and love for you. God is not asking you to be so strong, so perfect, so clean, and so pure. He is all those things. He is asking you to acknowledge that He has pulled out all the stops for you. He has planned your life of abundance. He has provided you with all your needs. He has given you the fruits of the spirit, and the gifts and talents you need. He has given you the armor to protect you. He has given you the weapons to fight with. He has given you freedom in salvation. He has written it all down for you. He has sent His one and only son to endure it all for you. He has endured it personally by becoming flesh for you. Now it is your turn. Will you get up and take this package that contains all your life and use it for the good of you and the good of many?

God knows what you are enduring, but he wants you to know He is enduring it all with you. When you hurt, He hurts. When you rejoice, He rejoices. You are one together, just like Him and Jesus. Take this time to study 1 Corinthians the chapter and learn how important you are and what all that you endure is for. Then begin a journal on what you are receiving as you read that book of the bible and watch how much you will grow and transform by the renewing of the mind.

ENDURE

Jill Deville

ABOUT THE AUTHOR

This book was written by Jill Deville after her fourth brain suregy in a two-year span. She learned through endurance there was a grand joy, peace, hope, faith, and healing, above all understanding that she would not have received without the perseverance and trust in the Lord. Jill writes these books to encourage others through her own personal journey with the Lord to be a witness that God can, and God will. We just need to not only know how to access Him, but we must also access Him with an action.

Jill is a country girl from Louisiana. Her greatest accomplishment is knowing Jesus and working for Him in her marriage, children, home, family, work, church, speaking events, and books. Jill strives to help people to know the word of God and how to apply the word of God in their lives. She has been with her husband for thirty-two years. Jill is a mother of three, one son, and two daughters. Her oldest children are married to their childhood sweethearts as well. Her youngest daughter is on fire for the Lord and right beside her as an ordained youth pastor at the age of 15. Jill is presently a grandmother of three, these three grandbabies keep her heart filled with joy.

By profession, Jill is a Senior Certified LDP and Senior Certified Mediator in the law field. She helps resolves family and civil matters in private. Her job fits her perfectly. God does say, " blessed are the peacemakers for they are children of God". She is also an Ordained Licensed Pastor of Gift Ministry of Louisiana a church she and her husband own and operate.

You can also stay connected and book events with Jill Deville on social media as Jill Deville World Ministry on all major social platforms. Her website is www.JillDevilleWorldMinistry.com.

Jill Deville World Ministry, expands the platform for Jesus to reach, teach, motivate, and excite others about the way, the truth, the life, Jesus Christ. Through this ministry she is a motivation speaker, author, publisher of her own books, and a teacher. Jill is a writer for sermons, bible studies, bible classes and her books. She travels the world for book signings, meet and greets, women's conferences, writers' conferences, bible studies, retreats, and even book clubs to interact with readers. Most of all she loves to get to know her brothers and sisters in Christ. She loves to speak and teach about God. More importantly she reveals the simplicity in such a way that helps readers to know this is not about works, religion, or status. We learn the word of God to get to know Jesus as a Father and a Friend. Jesus taught with parables and direct simplicity. He taught her this and she can not wait to share it with you.

OTHER TITLES
Show What You Know

Show What You Know is inspired by James 1:22 where James teaches us that knowing the word of God is not enough, we must do it. Show What You Know was written to assist you to learn the word of God with simplicity like Jesus taught. Show What You Know will assist you on getting to know Jesus, not just knowing of Him.

Show What You Know will help you to trade old actions and reactions for freeing actions and reactions that will bring peace, joy, hope, love and so much more. Show What You know is great for new Christians that are wondering, "what now" and "how do I apply this" without feeling defeated on day 1. Show What You Know will help Christians get back to quality time with Jesus to break free from religious works or excuses.

Jesus has a plan for us to prosper and succeed and we do not want to miss our blessing because we just do not see them. Show What You Know is great for a Bible Study or to help you learn how to study because it constantly refers you to God's word.

Jill Deville

The Inheritance

Are you tired of sharing your promises, opportunities, trauma, drama, dreams, hopes (pearls) only to have them torn to pieces by family, friends, and enemies (pigs & dogs) ? Do the things you say tend to get exaggerated, or become the talk of the town? Do you hear things like " why do you want to do that" or "you should do this?"

This book will encourage you that Jesus believes in you, chose you, and is there for you with a resolution. Be encouraged that He is your best yes, provider, listener, healer, and protector! Jesus has so many promises (pearls) for you. The Inheritance will remind you how precious your pearls are and how to pass them on to have the best Inheritance to give.

ENDURE

Armor Up

Armor Up, will help you to dig deep with simplicity. It frees you from religion and chore lists that make you feel defeated on day one. You will learn to put on God's armor and how to use it with this book. We have the equipment, the instructions, the directions, the armor, the promises, the examples and the map to get to Heaven (The Bible). Now together we just need to learn how to use it! When you are aware of the armor on you, nothing can harm you.

Jill Deville

THANK YOU

Thank you for your time, and support by reading Endure by Jill Deville. You truly are a blessing to God, and now to me too. If you enjoyed this book, write a review; so that together we can reach more people for Christ.

If you would like to book an event, such as a conference, motivational speaking engagement, book signing/ meet & greet, or even a book club. Count me in. I love working with Adults, Teens and Children for Jesus. I would love to connect with you. I also travel to preach and teach the word of God too. Contact me at JillDevilleWorldMinistry@gmail.com

For my schduele or to schduele go to Book It! Conferances & Events, God's Girls all through Jill Deville World Ministry on Facebook or my website at www.JillDevilleWorldMinistry.com.

Know that you are loved and Already Chosen.
With all the love of the Lord from me to you,

Jill Deville

Made in the USA
Coppell, TX
23 July 2024

35078354R10059